LOSING THE PHILIPPINES: ITS IMPACT ON OUR NATIONAL MILITARY STRATEGY FOR THE 90'S

INTRODUCTION

Since 1898, the Philippine Islands have been an important part of the United States' national military strategy for the Asian-Pacific region. Over time, this Pacific archipelago has served as a forward operating base, logistical and maintenance base, and a transportation hub for United States armed forces. Philippine bases have also supported the United States during four major wars this century: World War II, Korea, Vietnam, and Southwest Asian. Now, the United States will have to learn how to execute its Asian-Pacific foreign policy without the Philippines. With a reduced threat in the region and Philippine unwillingness to allow future United States basing, U.S. military presence within the region will change. To maintain a strong presence, the United States will have to use its remaining bases, its bilateral and multilateral treaties, and its naval capability to operate over extended distances.

This paper will provide an analysis of the U.S. military pullout from the Philippines and its effect on the United States' national military strategy in the Asian-Pacific region and the Philippines. First, I will discuss a brief history of the United States' presence in the Philippines, including policy for the region, goals, and activity. Next, I will evaluate the threat, including Philippine insurgency and external forces within the region. Finally, I will discuss current United States policy and strategy, as it relates to our changing world, and examine the United States military presence in the region without Philippine bases.

The end of the cold war has made many significant changes to world stability and peace. In particular, the United States' national military strategy must now confront a new group of threats. These threats will be characterized by regional conflicts in which the United States will be called upon to commit military forces to protect either its vital interests or its allies. To meet this challenge, the Chairman, Joint Chiefs of Staff, developed a new military strategy called the "Base Force Concept".[1]

In the Asian-Pacific region of the world, the United States' bases in the Philippines are a key element of this new military strategy. In the past, bases in Japan, South Korea, and the Philippines have formed the pillars of the United States' security umbrella over the Asian-Pacific region, protecting it from communism. More importantly, United States armed forces stationed in the Philippines are strategically located to protect the sea lines of communication that are so vital to United States national interests within the region. Mr. Paul Wolfowitz, Under Secretary of Defense for Policy, clearly articulated why our presence is important when he said:

"...our presence has contributed to regional peace and stability, by providing balance and insuring that no single state assumed a predominant military position. Our security presence has provided an environment in which nations could feel sufficiently confident of their own security, to turn away from militarism and authoritarianism, and toward democratic political systems and free market economies. Moreover, our global superpower status and our regional military presence have strengthened our influence in regional affairs."[2]

Philippine President Corazon Aquino's recent announcement that she was not going to fight her Senate's decision to extend United States basing rights in the Philippines created several unanswered questions concerning United States policy within the region. First, how will the pullout of United States forces in the Philippines effect United States national security policy and national military strategy within the Asian-Pacific realm? Next, how will the United States' pullout effect the Philippines' struggle to maintain a free and democratic nation? In particular, how will the United States' pullout effect the Philippines' fight against insurgency?

How the United States finds answers to these questions in the coming years will determine the extent to which we maintain our place as a world leader within the region. This paper will address these important questions and the nation's current military strategy's ability to meet the needs of the region in the 90's.

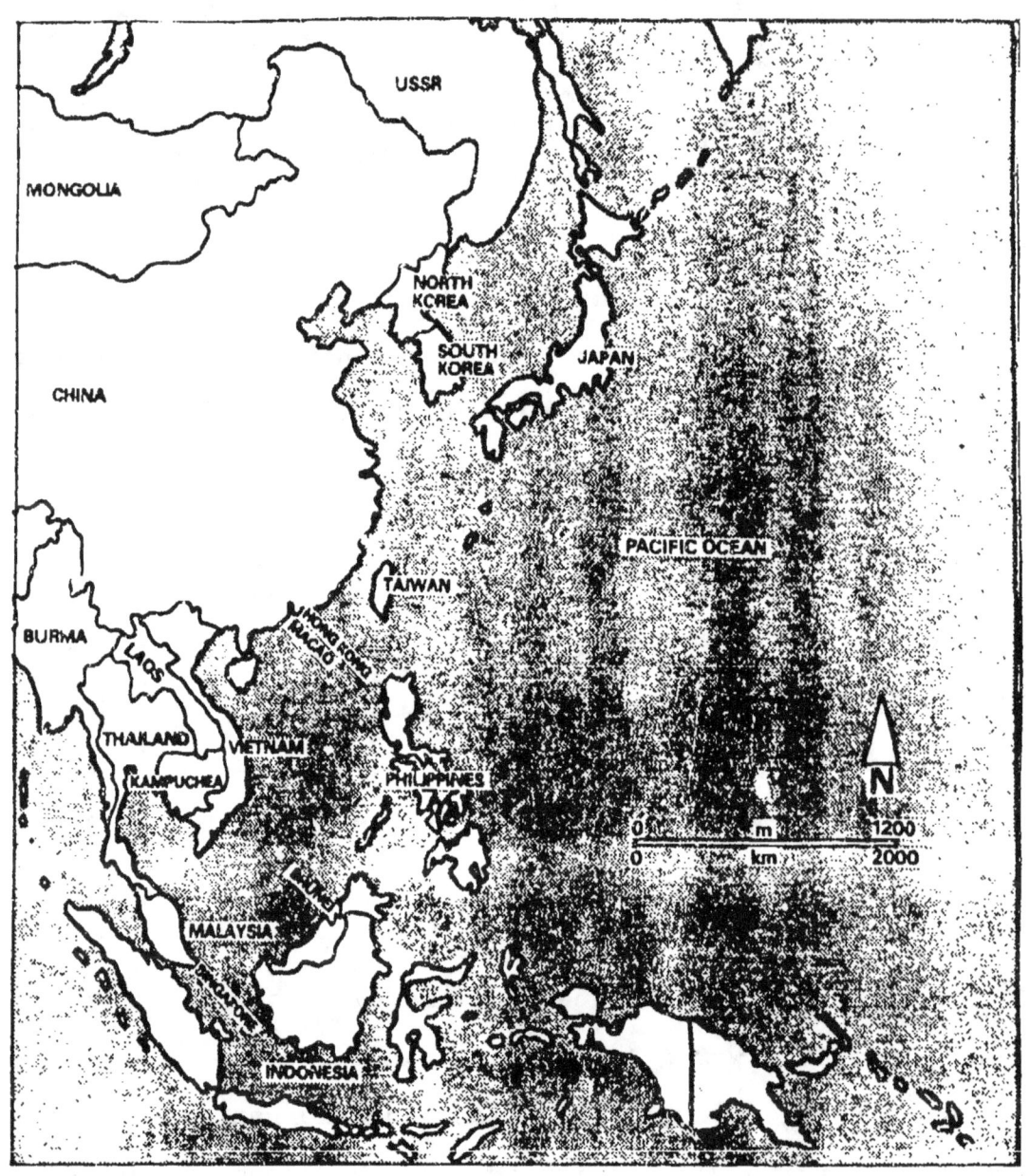

FIGURE 1. (ASIAN-PACIFIC REGION)

A HISTORICAL PERSPECTIVE

In order to understand current situations and relationships within the Asian-Pacific region, one needs a historical perspective of the United States' presence within the region, and particularly within the Philippines. As our nation was being born, Americans were looking toward the Pacific and the riches of Asia as a way of establishing the United States in the world. Great Americans like Thomas Jefferson, James K. Polk, Benjamin Harrison, William McKinley, and Commodores Perry and Dewey showed enormous courage and vision in opening the Pacific and Asia to American trade.[3]

In 1784, the United States took its first step toward opening trade routes in the Pacific and Asia when the ship, Empress of China, left Manhattan harbor and sailed for Canton, China. Encouraged by Thomas Jefferson and financed by Robert Morris, this voyage brought hopes of opening commerce and the riches of Asia to American business. The ship, loaded with furs and ginseng, left for China and returned with tea, china, and silk. More importantly, the United States was beginning to establish itself as an Asian-Pacific trading nation.[4]

By the turn of the century, American ships were expanding trade throughout the Pacific and Indian Oceans. Nations of the world were jockeying for positions of economic and military power within the region. Leading the way was Great Britain with her massive navy followed by France with her colonial desires. A series of less powerful nations, like the United States, were also aggressively trying to establish their places. The stakes were extremely high; in return for its investments, a nation received trade, territories (colonies), naval bases, and commercial treaties. These nations used their navies to forcibly open relatively defensive nations like Japan, China, and Korea to trade. Later, history would call this action, "gunboat diplomacy".[5]

The United States, like other nations, was also actively involved in "gunboat diplomacy". In 1852, Commodore Matthew Calbraith Perry with a squadron of four ships was ordered to open Japan to United States commerce and diplomacy. The real intent of this order was to meet British competition and secure for the United States a base of operations similar to the British base in Hong Kong.[6] In 1858, the United States and Japan signed a treaty which established United States diplomatic relations and naval bases within Japan. Of special note, the treaty also established the United States as Japan's protector while Japan modernized its nation and military forces--a job the United States would assume many years later following World War II. The treaty allowed Japan to buy arms, military equipment and supplies from the United States and to receive military training from United States advisors.[7]

During this period of time, Japan was not the only Asian nation to feel the weight of United States "gunboat diplomacy". In 1867, the United States Navy took Midway Island, and in 1871,

6

Marine and Naval forces successfully attacked Kanghoa Island, Korea.[8] By the start of Spanish-American War (1898), the United States had firmly established itself in the Pacific with national security interests that have lasted until today.

The Spanish-American War marked a turning point in United States influence within the Asian-Pacific region. As the nineteenth century came to a close, American consensus was split between governmental priorities. While some Americans thought that the federal government should concentrate on domestic issues, others (imperialists), like Theodore Roosevelt, Henry Cabot Lodge, and Captain Alfred Mahan, advocated a strong presence overseas. The imperialists of America believed that: "Only as a world power could the United States trade, prosper, and protect itself against its potential enemies...This role was America's manifest destiny.."[9] It was this prevailing imperialist philosophy which eventually caused the United States to fight the Spanish-American War and catapulted America's almost century-long involvement in the Philippines.

Strong public sentiment, adventurous businessmen, and a hawkish Congress, forced President William McKinley into war with Spain and sent United States soldiers to liberate Cuba. Concurrently, President McKinley ordered Commodore George Dewey to sink the Spanish fleet in Manila Bay and sent the first United States soldiers across the Pacific to occupy the Philippines.[10] At first, the United States did not want nor know what to do with the Philippines; but slowly, Americans began to dream of building an empire in the Pacific just as France, Britain, and Spain had done centuries earlier. American imperialists envisioned this Pacific archipelago as the center for trade within Asia and a means to establish the United States as a world power.[11]

Long before Commodore Dewey sailed into Manila Bay, the Filipino people were in the middle of their own fight for freedom with their Spanish masters. The Spanish brought Christianity and trade to the islands, but were also repressive and cruel masters to the Filipino people. Spain first turned the Philippines into a major trading port between Europe and China, and then, into an exporter of commodities like sugar. For over one hundred years prior the Commodore Dewey's arrival, the Filipinos had fought an off-and-on insurgency war with Spain.[12] Looking for help in their struggle for independence, Filipino insurgents, lead by Emilio Aguinaldo, assisted United States military forces in defeating the Spanish.

Initially, Filipinos believed that the United States had come to liberate the Philippines from Spain, but soon realized that they had been manipulated by Commodore Dewey and the United States. Filipino forces were not allowed to enter Manila, nor was Aguinaldo, self-proclaimed president of the Philippines, allowed to take control of the government. Tension between the United States and Filipino forces started to escalate. On February 4, 1899, fighting broke out in Manila.[13] A war that neither side really wanted would last for three years and would take a heavy toll on the Philippines.

To many Americans, this was a forgotten war--far from the United States; but in reality, this conflict was among the cruelest conflicts in American history. At its peak, 70,000 U.S. soldiers were involved; and by its end in 1901, at least 200,000 Filipino civilians had been killed.[14] Accounts of atrocities on both sides soured public opinion and resulted in the court-martial of U.S. Marine General Jacob Smith for war crimes against the Filipinos. The United States now had the Pacific colony that so many American imperialists wanted; but as a nation, America was losing its interest in colonialism.

The Treaty of Paris, which ended the Spanish-American War, signaled to the world that the United States was not only a world power, but also a Pacific power. In 1899, the United States regional power could be easily measured in terms of its territorial possessions: Puerto Rico, Guam, Samoa, Midway, Hawaii, and the Philippines. Additionally, the United States had established itself as a major trading nation within the Pacific-- with trade agreements in Japan, Korea, China, and other Asian nations. Future economic growth within the United States depended on trade in this region and more importantly, its critical sea lines of communication. The United States recognized the Asian-Pacific region to be an area of vital interests and stationed military forces within the region to protect those U.S. interests. The Philippines and Hawaii would soon become important players in the United States' future national military strategy.

9

Although the United States did not see itself as a colonial power, it did recognize the strategic military importance of the Philippines within the Asian-Pacific region. No sooner had the United States won its war in the Philippines than President McKinley started the process of preparing the Philippines for independence. To prepare the Philippines for self rule, the United States started a program of restoring order and reviving the economy. The program was lead by its first U.S. civilian governor, William Howard Taft.[15] Under Governor Taft's leadership, the Philippines were Americanized. He established governmental structure based on the fundamentals of democracy and built roads, schools, ports, and an American school system to educate Filipino children.[16] Many of today's Filipino governmental systems and organizations can be traced to Taft's initial programs.

After thirteen years as civilian governor of the Philippines, Taft was replaced by Frances Harrison whose progressive programs continued to prepare the Philippines for independence. He was responsible for introducing self government and Filipinization of civil service positions. In 1935, the United States granted the Philippines a commonwealth status with total independence scheduled for ten years later. As today, the plan required the United States to negotiate defense treaties and basing rights for U.S. military forces after independence.[17]

In 1941, when Japan attacked the United States in Hawaii and in the Philippines, the United States' plan for granting independence to the Philippines was interrupted. As a result of this war, the United States learned the importance of being an active world player, especially within the Asian-Pacific realm. No longer could the United States afford to sit on the sidelines as other nations, like Japan, set regional policy.

Following World War II, the major threats to the United States interests were the Soviet Union and the spread of communism.[18] No sooner had Japan surrendered, than Communism had started to blossom within the region in places like Vietnam, Korea, and China. As the free world's only superpower, the United States was the only Pacific nation with both the economic and military power to check communism. With numerous post-war military bases, such as the Philippines, Hawaii, Japan, Formosa, and Okinawa, the United States was also well positioned to support this massive undertaking.[19]

During the next forty plus years, the United States had to fight two wars (Korea and Vietnam) within the region to maintain its influence and check communism. Although historians may debate the United States' intent and lack of total victory, time has proven that these wars did contribute to suppressing communism and ultimately winning the cold war. Additionally, nations within the region continued to grow, trade prospered, and the sea lanes remained open. Key to this success was the United States' forward presence in the region and its military bases in the Philippines.

In 1946, as promised, the United States granted independence

to the Philippines. Along with independence, the United States
also signed a series of treaties that closely tied itself to the
new nation. These treaties included a ninety-nine year military
basing right's lease, continued economic trade provisions, and
tied the Philippines' currency to the dollar. Intended to
provide both national and economic security to the region and the
Philippines, the treaties in fact served to keep the island weak
and dependent upon the United States.[20].

Philippine problems with transitioning to independence and
its turbulent history since 1946 can be traced to flawed United
States policies during the years prior to independence. In
preparing the Filipinos for independence, United States civilian
governors had created a feudal system. For convenience purposes,
they had vested authority into a few wealthy, conservative
landowners and entrepreneurs. Over time, these individuals
resisted land, economic, and social reforms, thus creating
discontent and breeding insurgency.[21] Even today, less than one-
fifth of the Philippines' population receives over fifty percent
of the nation's income.[22] Following World War II, the United
States poured massive amounts of political and economic aid into
Japan, Korea, Formosa, and other Asian nations; yet, the United
States has done rather little, in comparison, to help its former
colony. Filipinos even today resent this fact.[23]

Since independence, the Philippines can best be described as
a nation dependent on the United States and having massive
poverty, corruption, and insurgency. This perception of the

Philippines was especially true during Ferdinand Marcos' administration (1965-1986). In looking for ways to bolster their economy and to stop internal strife, Filipinos have rekindled their nationalistic spirit and are trying to peacefully break their umbilical cord with the United States. When United States military forces leave the Philippines in the next couple of years, it will mark the first time in this century that the Philippines will not be a key element in U.S. national military strategy within the region.

Finally, history has shown that the United States is both a Pacific nation and power. The nation's economy, politics, and future are closely tied to events and issues within this important realm of the world. History has also shown that to be successful, the United States must be an active participant in regional affairs, and not one that sits back and allows other nations to establish regional policy. As in the past, the key to future United States regional participation will be the strength of its forward military presence.

AN EVOLVING THREAT WITHIN THE ASIAN-PACIFIC REGION

Since World War II, the United States has viewed the Soviet Union as its primary threat in the world and particularly within the Asian-Pacific realm. Along with the Soviet Union's demise in Europe, Soviet influence in the Asian-Pacific region has also diminished. The Pacific as well as the world is transforming itself from a bipolar region with two superpowers, the United States and the Soviet Union, into a region with many nations struggling for a position of power.[24] Since the collapse of the Soviet Union, the threat is not as easy to identify or articulate. Although a diminished threat, the Asian-Pacific realm does have a series of complex threats that potentially could make this theater one of the most dangerous in the President's "New World Order".

Because of its economic importance, the Asian-Pacific region, once a theater of economy of force, could easily become an area of vital interest to the United States. In his annual 1991 National Security Strategy document, President Bush said this about the region:

> "...East Asia and the Pacific are home to some of the world's most economically and politically dynamic societies. The region also includes some of the last traditional Communist regimes on the face of the globe. Regional hotspots tragically persist on the Korean peninsula and in Cambodia, and there are territorial disputes in which progress is long overdue..."[25]

Admiral Huntington Hardisty, Commander in Chief, U.S. Pacific Command described the threat within Asian-Pacific this way:

14

> "...Today, at last, we are entering a new era...Global tensions that might lead to nuclear war have been reduced...There are dangers ahead--in the world as a whole, and in the Pacific in particular, sources of potential regional instability abound...All of these dangers, as well as others none of us can foresee, exist in a region which is becoming the economic center of the world. Our own interests are totally intertwined with the money, markets, and resources of the Pacific. Our interdependence is such that regional instability could disrupt growth, alienate allies, and jeopardize our economic vitality..."[26]

This dynamic and complex region with new political, military, and economic threats will present many different and challenging problems for the United States' future policy-makers.

The Asian-Pacific realm is a region of the world which has problems as diverse as the nations who live within the region. These potentially destabilizing problems include ethnic strife, political instability, weapons proliferation, disparity of wealth, religious fundamentalism, narcotrafficking, terrorism, and insurgencies. In the past, the United States through its forward deployed presence within the region has provided the security umbrella which has ensured relative peace and prosperity. Now that the United States and the Soviet Union are reducing their presence in the region, the real threat is who will try to fill this vacuum.

Many nations within the region believe that a decline in the United States' presence would lead to a regional arms race involving Japan, North Korea, India, Vietnam, and China.[27] This view is not without merit, especially when one considers that the region is rich in natural resources, has some of the world's most

15

powerful economic nations, and has nine of the world's top twenty military powers.[28] This combination of economic wealth and military power could make Asia susceptible to threats of a single-nation dominance and thus, countering United States interests within the region.

In looking at the threats to the United States' interests within the region, three general areas of concern tend to surface: military threats, economic threats, and insurgencies. These three classifications of threats do not have the same magnitude as the Soviet Union did during the height of the cold war, but they do have the potential to effect regional stability. Conventional military threats within the region traditionally focus on North Korea, China, and Russia. More recently, India has also been mentioned as a possible military force within the region. The economic power within the region and the world is Japan. If access to its vital resources is threatened, or if as a nation it continues to build its conventional forces, Japan could become a destabilizing force. Insurgencies have always been a problem within the Asian-Pacific region. In particular, insurgencies in the Philippines, Indonesia, and Thailand have become important to regional security and unity.

Military Threats.

North Korea, despite the collapse of its major backer, the Soviet Union, continues to remain a threat within the region. It is still one of the world's most heavily armed nations, per

capita, in the world. In his testimony before the Senate Armed
Service Committee, General Lous C. Menetrey, USA, Commander, U.S.
Forces, Korea, described the North Korean threat:

> "...we see no evidence of glasnost or perestroika in
> North Korea, nor any plan to stop enlarging and
> modernizing its armed forces...Its revolutionary
> leadership, rigid ideology, Orwellian control over its
> citizens, make North Korea unpredictable and highly
> dangerous..."[29]

North Korea maintains the seventh largest standing armed forces
in the world and military expenditures average between 20 and 25
percent of its GNP.[30] Within one year, North Korea is expected
to become the region's second nuclear threat, with both the
technology and the means of delivering nuclear weapons. In
addition, North Korea is the major supporter of terrorism, arms
proliferation, and subversion within Asia.

The North Korean military was built at the expense of its
economy. Although North Korea's economy is failing and the
population living in despair, the nation's leadership is still
firmly in control. A failing economy and the loss of Soviet
support has forced North Korea to make peaceful overtones. It has
restarted peace talks with South Korea and has agreed to
inspection of its nuclear programs.[31] Despite these peaceful
overtones, North Korea continues to show aggressive behavior and
to be a destabilizing force in the region.

China, a traditional threat in the region, is a country of
vast power and influence, whose actions can affect the whole
region. In the past, China has been occupied with maintaining

17

its own internal security and reclaiming its lost territories of Hong Kong and Taiwan. Although China has shown signs of warming relations with the west, it is still determined to retain its communist government. Since Tiananmen Square, China's leadership has started to focus its efforts on eliminating its internal security threats and modernizing. To support its modernization programs, China has pursued a program of using foreign capital, technology, and expertise. Supporting its modernization programs, China has enlisted the help of the United States, Japan, Korea, and Western Europe.[32]

China's armed forces are the largest in the world, following the collapse of the Soviet Union, with over four million men in uniform.[33] By placing emphasis on air mobility, naval amphibious operations, and combined arms fighting, the Chinese military, the People's Liberation Army (PLA), has also continued to modernize its conventional forces. China's defense buildup has continued, uninterrupted, since 1979, focusing on research and development of equipment, nuclear weaponry, and space programs. China is the world's third largest nuclear force with the capability of hitting Kansas City with an ICBM carrying a five megaton warhead. China's space program has launched satellites and is now developing a more powerful rocket.[34]

Once China has solved its internal security problems, its economic and military growth could result in the nation refocusing its attention on external regional issues. In particular, China could be threatened by a shift of international power, the economic growth of Japan, Taiwan, and Korea, or brought into a border conflict with either Vietnam or India. China has the potential to control the Asian-Pacific region.

Although the cold war is over and the Soviet empire has crumbled, Russia still has a powerful military force. Its armed forces are large and modernized with the ability of projecting power into the region. If Russia solves its internal affairs, it could turn to the region to develop trade and to improve its economy. Russia has a long history of aggressive actions in Asia and should not be ruled out as a destabilizing regional force.

Economic Threats.

In a new world, where a nation's position of power is determined by its economic standing, one cannot evaluate the threat to national interests solely from a military perspective. The threat can also be defined in terms of economic power, trade relations, and availability of resources.[35] The Asian-Pacific realm of the world is no different. Many of the world's most dynamic economies are located within this region and are very susceptible in their ability to access raw materials, free sea lines of communication, and free world markets. These geographically small, yet economically giant nations include Japan, Taiwan, Singapore, Hong Kong, and more recentl South Korea. A perceived threat to one of these nations' economies could easily cause a major political or security problem for the region and the United States.

Japan, in particular, coupled with its enormous economic power, strong military force, and the mistrust of its neighbors is potentially a destabilizing force within the region. Although an economic superpower, Japan's weakness is that it is virtually dependent on other nations for all its raw materials. If Japan perceived a threat to its access of raw materials and trade, it could use its vast economic power and status as the world's banker to control the region. Currently, Japan is investing heavily into the following countries: Philippines, China, South and North Korea, and Indonesia.

What makes Japan a double threat is its world-class defense industry in the areas of aerospace, communications and electronics.[36] In 1990, Japan spent over twelve billion dollars on defense, one percent of its GNP, ranking it ninth in the world in military expenditures.[37] Japan, along with South Korea, North Korea, Singapore, Australia, Indonesia, and Taiwan, will soon turn the region into the major world producer of military arms. Additionally, Japan produces over eighty percent of its own military arms by using commercial technology for defense.[38]

Japan has also developed a very credible military defense force that defends its sea lines as far out as one thousand miles. Its military forces number over 240,000 and are highly trained and totally modernized with high-tech. equipment.[39] If Japan's defense policy and constitution were changed, allowing it to establish a formal military force, Japan could easily expand its industrial base and military force to meet its needs.

Because of Japan's economic aggression, actions of its officials, and its history of aggressive behavior during World War II, regional neighbors mistrust Japan's intentions and believe that it will become the biggest threat to regional security.[40]

Insurgencies.

Insurgencies are not new to the Asian-Pacific realm; they have been a destabilizing force since the West first started to colonize the region. Normally motivated by ethnic, ideological, or religious differences, insurgencies take the form of violent rebellions against established governments. To win popular support and sustain themselves, insurgent leaders develop campaigns that focus on the government's failure to alleviate social and economic problems such as poverty, human rights abuses, injustice, and corruption. The real threat from insurgencies comes from their influence on the region and their tendency to involve other countries. In recent times, Indonesia, Thailand, Malaysia, Vietnam, and Cambodia have had insurgencies.

Asia's longest running leftist insurgency has been in the Philippines. Filipino insurgents first fought their colonial masters (Spain, Britain, and America) and then the Japanese until the end of World War II. Following World War II, a communist-inspired rebellion lead by the Hukbalahaps (Huks) raged throughout the island until 1950. Insurgency operations were relatively quiet until 1965. Then Ferdinand Marcos and his repressive government came to power. Since 1965, with many different ethnic, religious, and ideologic groups participating, insurgencies have been a way of life within the Philippines.

Because of its diverse population, languages, and religions, the Philippines is a nation ripe for insurgencies. There are eight different main languages spoken on the islands, with a population consisting of Christian Filipinos, ethic Chinese, pagan tribes, and Muslim Filipinos.[41] Other than the communist, two other insurgency groups have been somewhat successful. The first is the Cordillera People's Liberation Army (CPLA) which is an ethnic minority insurgency; and, the second is the Moro National Liberation Front (MNLF) which is Muslim. Although these two insurgency groups have been somewhat quiet in recent years, they are potentially dangerous for the government.

The most threatening insurgency group is by far the communist with its extremely organized party. When the Huk's were defeated in 1950, the communist insurgents split into two groups: the Pro-Soviet Partido Komunista Philippines (PKP) and the pro-Chinese Communist Party of the Philippines (CCP). During the Marcos regime, the CCP with its military arm, the New People's Army (NPA), grew to become the most dangerous.[42]

A combination of communism's fall in Europe, China's Tiananmen, and effective counterinsurgency operations by the Corazon Aquino's government has weakened the CCP/NPA of late. The CCP's strength has been reduced from 25,000 in 1980, to around 17,500 in 1991. Although weakened, the CCP remains the most potent, long-term threat to stability within the Philippines

22

and influences daily life.[43] Most recently, the CCP/NPA has tied the withdrawal of U.S. military forces from the Philippines with a proposed ceasefire and peace talks.

The Filipino government's approach to dealing with the CCP/NPA and the policy of not renewing United States basing rights has caused a new fragment of rebellion from within the Philippine military. The emergence of three military insurgency groups, Reform the Armed Forces(RAM), Soldiers of the Filipino People(SFP), and Young Officer's Union(YOU), has resulted.in several coup attempts in recent years. These disgruntled soldiers are a powerful force with which the Filipino government is going to have to deal in the future.[44]

The problem of Filipino insurgency is a very serious regional issue. The Asian-Pacific community will sooner or later have to come to grips with this insurgency before it spreads to other nations. This type of situation is one that countries like Vietnam, China, and North Korea could easily exploit to achieve their own political and military objects.

The threat within the Asian-Pacific realm is transforming into one that could create instability and trouble for United States interests within the region. Characterized as military, economic, and insurgency in nature, these threats are just as real as the threats of the cold war. The challenge now for the United States is to first develop a regional security strategy and then develop a military strategy that both counters these threats and maintains American influence within the region.

REGIONAL SECURITY WITHOUT THE PHILIPPINES

As the threat and the role of the Philippines changes, so must the United States' military strategy change for the region. The United States' Asian-Pacific military strategy does not stand alone, but rather, is part of the nation's overall national military strategy. In looking at the United States' changing military strategy in the region, one must first look at the national military strategy.

United States military presence within the Asian-Pacific realm is based on United States national interests and objectives within the world. These national interests and objectives provide the framework by which the nation's national military strategy can be developed and applied on a regional basis. United States interests have not changed drastically and will probably remain the same in the future. The nation's four basic interests are: the survival of the United States as a free and independent nation; a healthy and growing U.S. economy; a healthy, cooperative, and vigorous relationship with our allies; and a stable and secure world, where political and economic freedom, human rights, and democracy can flourish.[45]

Each area of national interest has a series of objectives, twenty-one in all, which align with each interest and assist in establishing policy. The objectives which play an extremely important role in the Asian-Pacific realm are:

"-Prevent the transfer of militarily critical
technologies and resources to hostile countries;
-Ensure access to foreign markets, energy, mineral
resources, the oceans and space;
-Promote an open and expanding international economic
system, based on market principles;
-Maintain stable regional military balances to deter
those powers that might seek regional dominance;
-Aid in combatting threats to democratic institutions
from aggression, coercion, insurgencies, subversion,
terrorism and illicit drug trafficking;
-Support aid, trade and investment policies that
promote economic development and social and political
progress."[46]

Even though the United States' national interests and
objectives have not changed, the United States' national military
strategy is transforming. As in the past, the nation's military
strategy is based on the foundation of deterrence, but now is
using the concepts of forward presence, crisis response, and
force reconstitution.[47] What is also new is the way the JCS
intends to counter regional threats using General Powell's "Base
Force" concept (figure 2).

The base force concept is a unique concept, developed to
counter complex regional threats while maximizing dwindling
defense resources. In practice, the concept uses small forward
deployed forces in the Pacific and Atlantic theaters. These
forces are backed by a strong, highly mobile contingency force in
the United States. This contingency force is designed to quickly
reinforce any theater of operation with either light or heavy
forces. Supporting these forward deployed and contingency forces
are four supporting capabilities: space, research, development
and acquisition, transportation, and reconstitution.[48]

BASE FORCE CONCEPT

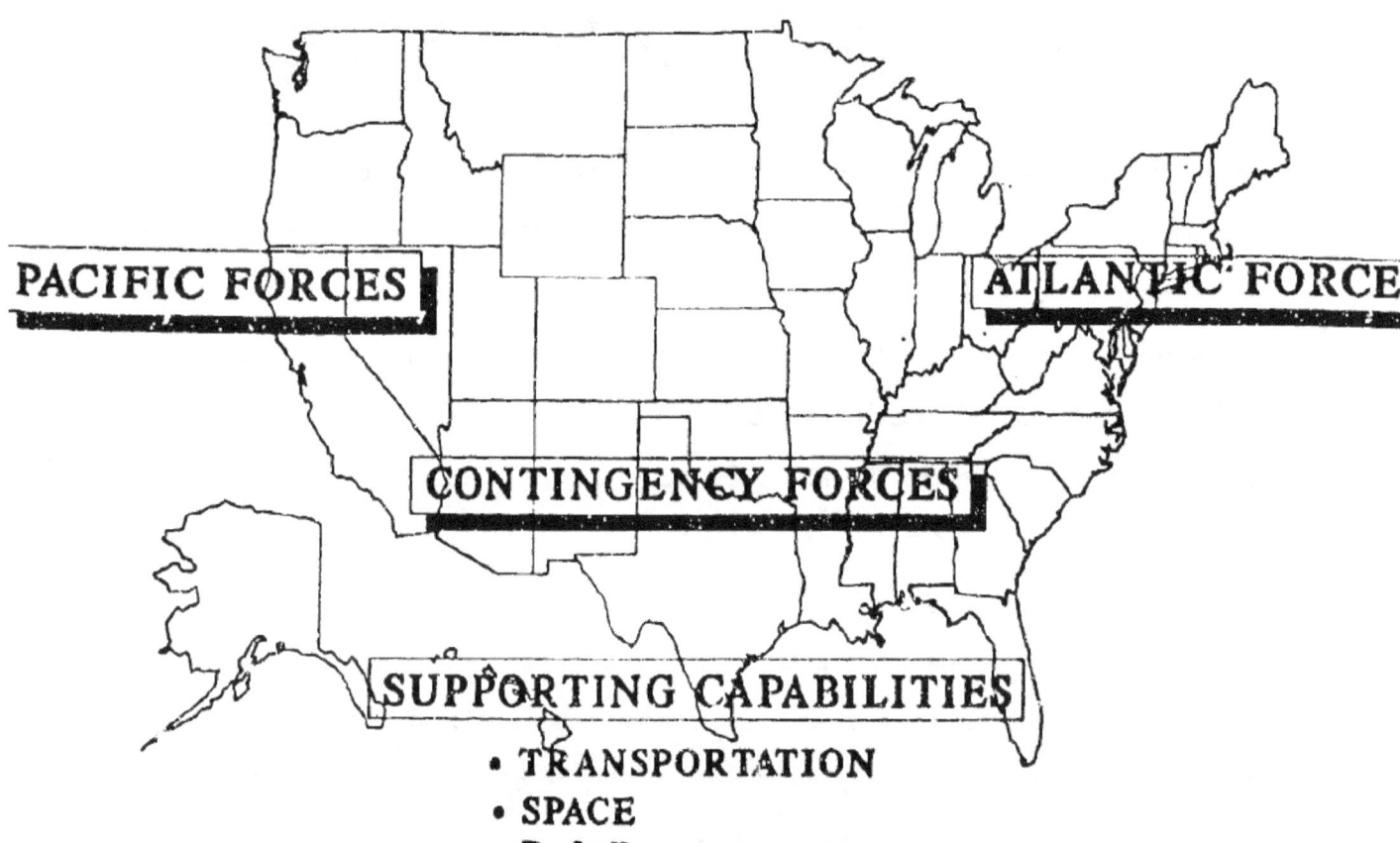

STRATEGIC FORCES

PACIFIC FORCES

ATLANTIC FORCES

CONTINGENCY FORCES

SUPPORTING CAPABILITIES

- TRANSPORTATION
- SPACE
- R & D
- RECONSTITUTION

FIGURE 2. (BASE FORCE CONCEPT)

The utility of this concept is that it provides forward presence throughout the world while the nation's combat power is being consolidated and readied to respond to a crisis.

In a world threatened by a superpower like the former Soviet Union, the Philippines has and would play an extremely important role in the United States' forward presence in the region. Philippine airfields, training facilities, logistical bases, and natural naval harbors offer excellent facilities for forward deployed U.S. military forces. Now that the cold war has ended and the regional threat is somewhat less sophisticated, the Philippines' facilities take on a less important role. To prevent one nation from becoming the single-dominant force in the region, the United States must continue to use forward military presence to maintain its place as a Pacific power.

Using the base force concept in executing national military strategy, the United States will need fewer military forces within the Asian-Pacific region to provide forward presence. The requirement to provide logistic and maintenance bases, training facilities, and trans-shipment points for equipment and personnel can be accomplished without the Philippines. Forward presence does not mean that large combat forces need to be permanently stationed within the Asian-Pacific realm. The United States can use other means to achieve its strategy, such as a series of smaller support bases, bilateral and multilateral defense treaties, joint and combined training exercises, and the U.S. Navy maneuvering within the region to accomplish its forward

27

presence mission.

The major advantage, in the past, of using the Philippines as a logistical base and repair/overhaul facility has been its strategic location and cheap labor. In today's world, the United States has many more options available for accomplishing these same functions for its smaller forward deployed forces. Without the Philippines, the United States can use other strategic locations like Singapore, Thailand, Japan, Korea, and Guam. Although the cost of repairs at these locations will be more than those of the Philippines, the costs are still much less than those in the continental United States or Hawaii. The best course of action would be to spread the support requirements among three or four smaller bases within the region. The work at these bases could be contracted out to save money and be manned by small detachments of U.S. military personnel, similar to the United States' arrangement with Singapore.[49]

In line with establishing support bases throughout the region, the United States needs to also continue its practice of establishing bilateral and multilateral treaties with the Asian-Pacific nations. Because of the many ethnic, religious, and cultural differences among the nations of this region, there is no regional institution like NATO to provide the framework for regional stability. Bilateral and multilateral treaties are the only form of establishing political and defensive cooperation within the region and preventing single-nation domination.

These treaties should tie the defense requirements of these

nations to United States interests and objectives for the region. The treaties should include requirements that provide for aircraft landing rights, naval facilities usage, and storage sites for wartime material and supplies, similar to what the United States has in other parts of the world. If a conflict erupts in the Asian-Pacific area or another area of the world, these stocks and facilities could be used with permission of the host country to support U.S. military operations. These sites would be small and non-threatening to a nation and at the same time show United States presence in the country.

One of the best ways of demonstrating forward presence and multinational cooperation is to conduct military training exercises throughout the region. These exercises could emulate the ones that the United States does in Korea, Thailand, and Australia. The training exercises can be as small as either a single Navy ship or an Air Force fighter squadron, or as large as either an Army Division or a Navy Carrier Battle Group. An example of this type of cooperation is in the training of air combat crews. In losing the Philippines, the United States gave up one of the best air combat ranges in the region, the Crow Valley range. Through defense agreements or treaties, a regional air combat range could be established in several places like Indonesia, Thailand, or even at Crow Valley. Jointly run and funded, nations of the region could rotate their air crews through this range for quality training.

Lastly, the U.S. Navy can provide United States presence

within the region by doing what it has done for over one hundred years, conducting freedom of navigation throughout the Pacific realm. For years, United States ships sailing in and out of ports within the region have been a sign of American influence and power. Recent advancements in technology have provided the United States Navy with the capability of operating for large periods of time without needing permanent overseas bases.[50] This capability now allows American ships and fleets to operate out of bases in Hawaii and the United States while continuing to reach all parts of the Asian-Pacific realm. A time tested and proven concept, naval maneuvers coupled with various small support bases, security treaties, and joint military exercises will provide the credible presence the United States needs for protecting its national interests and security within Asia-Pacific.

CONCLUSION

The United States has emerged from the cold war as the world's only true economic and military superpower. To stay on top of this dynamic and changing world, the United States is transforming its national military strategy. Going away from the traditional threat within Central Europe, strategists are looking more toward the Pacific as the key to United States security and economic well-being. The United States has and will remain a Pacific nation whose power and national interests are intertwined with those of the Asian-Pacific nations. How the United States projects its presence within the region will determine the United States' position at the bargaining table during future economic and political negotiations.

The Asian-Pacific region of the world has, since 1784, been extremely important to the United States' economy and well-being. As a nation, the United States has developed into a superpower based, in part, on its military and economic influence within the region. Initially, using "gunboat diplomacy", the United States helped to open the region to world trade; then, as a colonial power, the United States helped develop and industrialize the region. Following World War II, the United States, now a superpower, provided security and helped to rebuild the war-torn region. Even as America's past has been intermeshed with this important part of the world, so will its future be closely linked to the region's political and economical stability.

Since the fall of the Berlin Wall and communism in Eastern Europe, the threat within the Asian-Pacific realm has changed from a simple one, between two superpowers, to a complex one. The United States must now come to grips with conventional threats, economic threats, and insurgencies. More importantly, the combination of economic wealth and military power makes this region susceptible to single-nation dominance and counters United States interests within the region. The Asian-Pacific realm has many potentially destabilizing problems which, if left unchecked, could involve the United States in an armed conflict to protect either its interests or its allies. Although a reduced threat, the threats within the Asian-Pacific region are real and extremely dangerous to United States security and its well-being as a superpower nation.

The key to countering this real but complex threat is to deter single-nation dominance through United States military presence within the region. The concept of forward presence does not necessarily mean large military forces stationed within the region in places like the Philippines. The real intent of forward presence is to provide within the region the appropriate size military forces to deter conflict, protect regional national interests, and project influence. In today's world environment, a smaller, but highly mobile forward deployed force that can be quickly reinforced from bases within the United States can accomplish this mission--a job traditionally handled by the U.S. Navy for centuries.

With the cold war at an end, the regional threat somewhat less sophisticated, and U.S. armed forces downsizing, the Philippines dons a less important role in U.S. military strategy for the region. Although the United States will continue to use forward presence to prevent single-nation dominance of the region, the United States can use means, other than the Philippines, to achieve its regional military strategy. In particular, the United States can rely on bilateral and multilateral treaties, a series of smaller support bases within the region, joint/combined training exercises, and the U.S. Navy sailing throughout the region to accomplish its forward presence mission. The Philippines has been an important part of our nation's history. However, it is now time to allow the Philippines to pursue its own course and prevent the United States' regional security strategy from being unnecessarily tied to this Pacific nation.

ENDNOTES

1. Chairman, Joint Chiefs of Staff. Speech, Statement of General Colin Powell Before the Senate Armed Services Committee, Alderson Reporting Company, 1991, 44.

2. U.S. Congress. Senate, Committee on Armed Services. The President's Report on the U.S. Military Presence in East Asia. Hearing before the Committee on Armed Services, 101st Cong., 2d Sess., (April 29, 1990): 13.

3. Richard O'Connor. Pacific Destiny: An Informal History of the U.S. in the Far East (Boston: Little, Brown and Co, 1969), ix.

4. Ibid., 24-26.

5. Ibid., 104-105.

6. Ibid., 109.

7. Ibid., 116.

8. Ibid., 141.

9. Stanley Karnow. In Our Image: America's Empire in the Philippines (New York: Random House, 1989), 10.

10. Ibid., 102.

11. Ibid., 11.

12. Lea E. Williams. Southeast Asia: A History (New York: Oxford University Press, 1976), 135-137.

13. Karnow. In Our Image. 12.

14. Ibid., 12.

15. O'Connor. Pacific Destiny. 284.

16. Karnow. In Our Image. 172-177.

17. Russell H. Fifield. Americans in Southeast Asia: The Roots of Commitment (New York, Thomas Y. Crowell, Co, 1973), 8-9.

18. Ibid., 58.

19. O'Connor. Pacific Destiny. 458.

20. Williams. Southeast Asia: A History. 206.

21. Karnow. In Our Image. 198.

22. Ibid., 22.

23. Ibid., 23.

24. Thomas L. Wilborn, "How Northeast Asians View Their Security," Strategic Studies Institute, U.S. Army War College (8 August 1991): vii.

25. President, National Security Strategy of the United States (Washington, D.C.: GPO, 1991), 9.

26. Huntington Hardisty, Adm. U.S. Navy, "A Long-Term Game Plan," Change, Interdependence and Security in the Pacific Basin: The 1990 Pacific Symposium, National Defense University Press, Washington, D. 1991, 5-7.

27. Sheldon W. Simon, "U.S. Interests in Southeast Asia," Asian Survey (July 1991): 671.

28. George Thomas Kerion, The New Book of World Rankings, 3d Edition, (Facts on File, Inc. 1991), 58-63.

29. U.S. Congress. Senate, Committee on Armed Services. Threat Assessment; Military Services and Operational Requirements, Hearing before the Committee on Armed Services, 101st Cong., 2d Sess., (22 March 1990): 499-503.

30. Kurion, The New Book of World Rankings, 57-61.

31. Barbara Crossette, "U.S.-North Korea Talks Planned on State of Nuclear Development," The New York Times, January 15, 1992, A12.

32. Parris H. Chang, Dr., "China and the Great Powers to the Year 2000," Change, Interdependence, and Security in The Pacific Basin: The 1990 Pacific Symposium," (National Defense University Press, 1991), 33.

33. Kurion, The New Book of World Ranking, 58.

34. Chong-Din Lin, "Taiwan and China After Tiananmin: Dialectics in Future Relations," Changes, Interdependence and Security in the Pacific Basin: The 1990 Pacific Symposium, (National Defense University Press, 1990), 63-64.

35. Bradford, "Asia-Pacific Policy: A Review of the Literature," The Washington Post, Spring 1990, 200.

36. Doug Joon Hwang, "Regional Arms Production, Cooperation and Pacific Security," Change, Interdependence and Security in The Pacific Basin: The 1990 Pacific Symposium, (National Defense

35

University Press, 1990), 124.

37. Kurion, The New Book of World Rankings, 61.

38. Hwang, "Regional Arms Production Cooperation and Pacific Security," 124-128.

39. Kurion, The New Book of World Rankings, 58.

40. Wilborn, "How Northeast Asians View Their Security," 50-51.

41. DA Pamphlet 550-72, "Area Handbook for Philippines," Washington, D.C., American University, 1982, vii.

42. Richard G. Stilwell, "Averting Disaster in the Philippines," Policy Review, Winter 1988, 20.

43. S. Bilver, "The U.S. without Clark Air Base: Its meaning and Implications," Asian Defence, September 1991, 94.

44. "Philippines," Asia 1991, 1991, 197.

45. National Security Strategy of the United States, 3-4.

46. Ibid., 3-4.

47. National Security Strategy of the United States, 25.

48. Statement of General Colon Powell Before the Senate Armed Service Committee, 44-48.

49. John E. Young, "Bush Eyes Accord With Singapore," The Washington Post, 4 January 1992, A13.

50. Michael Richardson, "Life After Subic," Asia-Pacific Defence Reporter, November 1991, 31-32.

BIBLIOGRAPHY

Alves, Dora, ed. Changes, Interdependence and Security in the Pacific Basin. Washington, D.C.: National Defense University Press, 1991.

Bilver, S. Dr. "The U.S. without Clark Air Base: Its Meaning and Implications." Asian Defence (September 1991): 26-98.

Bradford, David G. "Asia-Pacific Policy: A Review of the Literature." The Washington Quarterly (Spring 1990): 197-210.

Chairman, Joint Chiefs of Staff. Speech. Statement of General Colin Powell Before the Senate Armed Service Committee. Washington, D.C.: Alderson Reporting Company, 1991.

Crossette, Parris H. "U.S.-North Korea Talks Planned on State of Nuclear Development." The New York Times, 15 January 1992, A12.

DA Pamphlet. "Area Handbook for Philippines." Washington, D.C.: American University, 1982.

Fifield, Russell H. Americans in Southeast Asia: The Roots of Commitment. New York: Thomas Y. Crowell Company, 1973.

Gordon, Bernard K. New Directions for American Policy in Asia. New York: Routledge, Chapman and Hall, Inc, 1990.

Karnow, Stanley. In Our Image: American's Empire in the Philippines. New York: Random House, 1989.

Kurion, George Thomas. The New Book of World Rankings. 3d ed. New York: Facts on File, Inc., 1991.

Morrison, Charles E. Threats to Security 'n East Asia-Pacific. Lexington Books, 1983.

Myers, David J. Regional Hegemons: Threat Perceptions and Strategic Response. Boulder, Co.: Westview Press, 1991.

New Political-Military Realities in East Asia: An Assessment of U.S. Interests, Threats and Commitments. Strategic Studies Institute, U.S. Army War College: 1990.

O'Connor, Richard. Pacific Destiny: An Informal History of the U.S. in the Far East. Boston: Little, Brown and Co., 1969.

"Philippines." Asia 1991, 1991.

Richardson, Michael. "Life After Subic." Asia-Pacific Defence Reporter. xviii, no. 5. (November 1991): 31-32.

Sales, Peter M. "Social Volcano Still Smouldering." Asia-Pacific Defense Reporter. xviii, no. 6/7. (Dec/Jan 92): 28-31.

Simon, Sheldon W. "U.S. Interests in Southeast Asia." Asian Survey. (July 1991): 662-675.

Stilwell, Richard G. "Averting Disaster in the Philippines." Policy Review. Winter 1988.

Strategic Survey 1990-1991. The International Institute for Strategic Studies. New Jersey: Brassey's, Inc., May 1991.

Tahir-Khili, Shirin. U.S. Strategic Interest in Southwest Asia. New York: Praeger Publishers, 1982.

Tow, William T. Encountering the Dominant Player. New York: Columbia University Press, 1991.

U.S. Congress. Senate. Committee on Armed Services. Threat Assessment; Military Strategy; and Operational Requirements: Hearing before the Committee on Armed Services. 101st Cong., 2d Sess., 22 March 1990.

U.S. Congress. Senate. Committee on Armed Services. The President's Report on the U.S. Military Presence in East Asia: Hearing Before The Committee on Armed Services. S.HRG 101-880, 101st Cong., 2d Sess., 19 April 1990.

U.S. President. National Security Strategy of the United States. Washington, D.C: GPO, August 1991.

Wilborn, Thomas L. "How Northeast Asians View Their Security." Strategic Studies Institute, U.S. Army War College, 1991.

Williams, Lea E. Southeast Asia: A History. New York: Oxford University Press, 1976.

Young, John E. "Bush Eyes Accord With Singapore." The Washington Post, 4 January 1992, A13.